RACING SPORTS

FORMULA 1 RACING

BY DALTON RAINS

WWW.APEXEDITIONS.COM

Apex is distributed by North Star Editions:
sales@northstareditions.com | 888-417-0195

Produced for Apex by Red Line Editorial.

Photographs ©: Mark Baker/AP Images, cover; Michael Probst/AP Images, 1, 22–23; Hoch Zwei/picture-alliance/dpa/AP Images, 4–5, 14, 29; Ryan Remiorz/The Canadian Press/AP Images, 6–7; Michael Conroy/AP Images, 8–9; Eddie Worth/AP Images, 10–11; STF/AP Images, 12–13; Claude Paris/AP Images, 15; Eurico Rodriguez/Dreamstime, 16–17; John Crouch/Icon Sportswire/AP Images, 18; Shutterstock Images, 19, 20–21; Anthony Behar/Sipa USA/AP Images, 24–25; Steven Tee/Motorsport Images/Sipa USA/AP Images, 26–27

Library of Congress Control Number: 2022923787

ISBN
978-1-63738-536-4 (hardcover)
978-1-63738-590-6 (paperback)
978-1-63738-696-5 (ebook pdf)
978-1-63738-644-6 (hosted ebook)

Printed in the United States of America
Mankato, MN
082023

NOTE TO PARENTS AND EDUCATORS

Apex books are designed to build literacy skills in striving readers. Exciting, high-interest content attracts and holds readers' attention. The text is carefully leveled to allow students to achieve success quickly. Additional features, such as bolded glossary words for difficult terms, help build comprehension.

TABLE OF CONTENTS

CHAPTER 1

START YOUR ENGINES

The Formula 1 cars **rev** their engines at the starting line. When the green flag waves, they roar onto the track.

Drivers try to get into a good position early in the race.

One driver starts out ahead. But another driver quickly takes the lead. It is a close race.

Passing another driver is not easy. Drivers carefully plan their moves.

POLE POSITION

In Formula 1, drivers compete in **qualifying** rounds before races. The driver with the fastest time gets the best position at the front. This spot makes it easier to win the race.

A checkered flag waves when the winner crosses the finish line.

The drivers turn into the final lap. They are still close. Then one driver slides ahead. His car crosses the finish line. He wins!

FAST FACT

Formula 1 races are at least 190 miles (305 km) long.

CHAPTER 2

FORMULA 1 HISTORY

In the early 1900s, people started **Grand Prix** racing. They formed racing clubs. Some clubs decided to join together. They agreed on a set of rules called Formula 1.

Early races often took place on long routes between cities.

Later, the clubs created a world **championship.** It first took place in 1950. Drivers earned points across seven races.

Drivers using Alfa Romeo cars won the first two Formula 1 titles.

FAST FACT

Formula is a word for styles of racing and their rules. The number 1 means it's the top level.

Today, more than 20 Formula 1 races happen each year. People all over the world follow the popular sport.

Each year, millions of people attend Formula 1 races in person.

The Monaco Grand Prix was first held in 1929.

FAMOUS RACE

One of the most famous Formula 1 races is the Monaco Grand Prix. The track for this race twists around city streets. It also goes through tunnels.

CHAPTER 3

HOW IT WORKS

There are 10 teams in Formula 1. Each team has two drivers. Each **season**, they compete in Grand Prix races around the world.

Drivers line up in their starting positions before the race begins.

Formula 1 races last two hours or less. The races end even if some drivers haven't finished.

The top 10 drivers in each race get points. When the season ends, the driver with the most points is the champion.

FAST FACT

Michael Schumacher was one of the best Formula 1 drivers. He won 91 races.

Max Verstappen was the Formula 1 World Drivers' Champion for the 2021 season.

Drivers' scores are added together for a team score, too. The top team wins the Constructors' Championship.

Top teams include Red Bull, Mercedes, and Ferrari.

LOTS OF LAPS

Formula 1 drivers race around **circuits**. Most races have 50 to 70 laps. Each circuit is a different length and shape. But all have long straight parts and sharp corners.

CHAPTER 4

EQUIPMENT

Each Formula 1 team builds its own cars. They make the cars as fast as possible. The cars have powerful engines.

Formula 1 cars can go up to 235 miles per hour (378 km/h).

Formula 1 cars have wings at the front and the back. These parts help air move around the cars without slowing them down.

FAST FACT

Formula 1 cars can cost more than $20 million to make.

A Formula 1 car's shape helps it go fast.

Formula 1 drivers wear clothes that won't catch fire. Their gloves have **biosensors**. They track drivers' heart rates and **stress** levels. That helps the drivers stay safe.

PIT CREWS

During races, drivers sometimes pull over for pit stops. That's when pit crews add fuel or make fast fixes to the cars. They can change all four tires in two seconds or less.

Each driver's helmet is created just for them.

COMPREHENSION QUESTIONS

Write your answers on a separate piece of paper.

1. Write a few sentences that explain the main ideas of Chapter 2.

2. Would you want to drive a Formula 1 car? Why or why not?

3. Which parts help move air around a car without slowing it down?

- **A.** biosensors
- **B.** engines
- **C.** wings

4. Why do Formula 1 drivers wear helmets?

- **A.** to check their heart rates and stress levels
- **B.** to talk with other drivers on their teams
- **C.** to avoid getting hurt if they crash

5. What does **compete** mean in this book?

*Each team has two drivers. Each season, they **compete** in Grand Prix races around the world.*

A. race
B. watch
C. leave

6. What does **champion** mean in this book?

*When the season ends, the driver with the most points is the **champion**.*

A. slow driver
B. winner
C. loser

Answer key on page 32.

GLOSSARY

biosensors
Devices that measure signals or changes in the body, such as a person's heart rate.

championship
A contest that decides a winner.

circuits
Looped tracks of road where races happen.

Grand Prix
A car race on a difficult course that is part of a world championship series.

qualifying
Types of earlier races used to pick where drivers will start in later races.

rev
To make an engine speed up and work harder.

season
The series of Formula 1 races that take place each year.

stress
The body and mind's responses to difficult situations.

TO LEARN MORE

BOOKS

Cain, Harold P. *Lewis Hamilton*. Lake Elmo, MN: Focus Readers, 2023.

Hamilton, S. L. *The World's Fastest Cars*. Minneapolis: Abdo Publishing, 2021.

Rechner, Amy. *Race Car Driver*. Minneapolis: Bellwether Media, 2020.

ONLINE RESOURCES

Visit **www.apexeditions.com** to find links and resources related to this title.

ABOUT THE AUTHOR

Dalton Rains is a writer and editor from St. Paul, Minnesota. He loves spending time outdoors and learning about all kinds of sports.

INDEX

ANSWER KEY:

1. Answers will vary; 2. Answers will vary; 3. C; 4. C; 5. A; 6. B